Animal Safari Nature Library

Elephant Herds and Rhino Horns

by Don Arthur Torgersen

Photographs by Lee Trail
and Don Torgersen

Consulting Editor
Gilbert K. Boese, Ph.D.
Director
Milwaukee County Zoo

CHILDRENS PRESS, CHICAGO

Acknowledgments

The author would like to thank the following institutions for assistance given in the development of this series: Chicago Zoological Society and Brookfield Zoo, Lincoln Park Zoo, Field Museum of Natural History, Milwaukee County Zoo, Minnesota Zoological Garden, St. Louis Zoo, Denver Zoo, San Diego Zoo, West Palm Beach Zoo, Lion Country Safari, Miami Seaquarium, Crandon Park Zoological Gardens on Key Biscayne, Sea World, National Zoological Park in Washington, D.C., Worthley N.L. Burbank Nature Center.

Project Editor: Joan Downing

Library of Congress Cataloging in Publication Data

Torgersen, Don Arthur, 1934-
  Elephant herds and rhino horns.

  (Animal safari nature library)
  SUMMARY: Text and photographs feature the physical characteristics, territories, feeding habits, and behavior in the wild and in zoos of the world's largest land mammals, including elephants, rhinos, river hippopotamuses, and tapirs.
  1. Ungulata—Juvenile literature. 2. Elephants—Juvenile literature. 3. Mammals—Juvenile literature.
[1. Ungulates. 3. Mammals] I. Trail, Lee, ill. II. Title. III. Series: Torgersen, Don Arthur, 1934-Animal safari nature library.
QL737.U4T67   599.3   81-10158
ISBN 0-516-00652-5   AACR2

  3 4 5 6 7 8 9 10 11 12 R 89 88 87 86 85 84 83

Contents

*A young elephant likes to have
its tongue tickled.*

African elephants are social animals that live in large herds.

World's Largest Land Animals

Elephants, rhinos, and hippos are the world's largest land animals. With tapirs, they belong to a group of animals called *pachyderms*—thick-skinned animals. But otherwise, they are not closely related.

Their ancestors were even larger animals. These huge creatures once roamed many parts of the world. Now most of the world's largest land animals live only in Africa and parts of Asia.

In the wild, most of these large mammals usually live in groups or herds. But a few live as solitary individuals. The herds need large areas of land, many rivers and lakes, and a constant supply of plant food. All of the large land mammals are *herbivores*, or plant-eating animals. They do not eat meat. They are browsers and grazers. They eat mainly plant matter taken from grasses, shrubs, bushes, leaves, and trees.

The large land mammals also live and breed in zoos. Zoo keepers provide the animals with food, water, and health care. Their zoo diets are usually more constant than their diets in the wild. They are fed hay, oats, herbs, fruits, vegetables, breads, and special vitamins. The animals usually live long, comfortable lives in zoos.

5

Hippos, rhinos, and elephants like to roll and wallow in mud. The mud helps to keep their bodies cool. The mud also protects them from the bites of flies, ticks, and other insects. Tick birds often stand on the backs and heads of these large animals. The birds peck at ticks and other pests with their beaks.

All plant and animal life is related. Human beings need a wide variety of plant and animal life to exist. It is important to learn about animals, their environments, and the way they live.

People have always been curious about animals. Wild animals have attracted naturalists, scientists, environmentalists, writers, and photographers. They have also attracted the deadliest of all creatures—the big-game hunter.

The large mammals of Africa and Asia have seldom been dangerous to human beings. But big-game hunters have killed thousands upon thousands of these animals with high-powered rifles—simply for sport.

A large African elephant amuses people at a zoo.

Elephants—The Big Tuskers

The elephant is the largest of all land animals. Some bull elephants stand twelve feet tall at the shoulders and weigh more than twelve thousand pounds. One very large African male measured thirteen feet, two inches high at the shoulders. He weighed fourteen thousand pounds. Most adult male elephants are ten to eleven feet tall and weigh between ten thousand and twelve thousand pounds. Female elephants are smaller.

Even though an elephant has great size, it can move quickly and has very good balance. An elephant can run faster than a man for short distances. A few have been timed running twenty-five miles per hour.

There are two *species* of elephants. One is the *African elephant*, which is widespread throughout Africa. It is found in the tropical forests, on the grassy *savannas*, and along the river valleys.

The other species is the *Asian elephant*. It lives in the thick tropical forests of India, Burma, Thailand, and Sri Lanka.

There are important differences between African and Asian elephants. Their tooth structure, body shape, and habits are different. African elephants are taller than Asian elephants and often live in larger herds. Male and female African elephants have longer tusks. Some female Asian elephants grow very short tusks called *tushes* that hardly can be seen at all.

African elephants have huge ears. Some people think that these ears are shaped like maps of Africa. Asian elephants have smaller ears.

Asian elephants have been *domesticated*. That means they are useful to people. Female Asian elephants are easier to handle and train than all other elephants. They are usually the elephants used in circuses. Asian elephants also have been used to carry teakwood logs out of the forests where they are cut.

*The African elephant has large
ears and a sloping forehead.*

*Asian elephants have smaller
ears and knobby heads.*

Elephants drink between thirty and fifty gallons of water each day.

In Africa and in Asia, elephant herds are made up of many related family groups. Adult females lead the herd and take care of the young. Adult males follow the herd but do not mix with females except during mating times.

As plant eaters, elephants require an enormous amount of food. They spend more than half their lives eating. African elephants often browse on the sunny savannas for food. Asian elephants do not like to browse in sunlight. They prefer the heavy cover of forest trees.

Elephants browse from tree to tree, eating bark, leaves, twigs, branches, and fruit. They pull their food down with their long trunks. They also eat grasses and even the roots of some trees. A wild elephant eats between five hundred and seven hundred pounds of food each day.

Elephants in zoos eat between one hundred and two hundred pounds of food each day. They do not get as much exercise as elephants in the wild. So their appetites are not as great.

Elephants in the wild drink between thirty and fifty gallons of water daily. In dry seasons, when riverbeds are very shallow and water levels are low, many of the older elephants dig wells. They kick at the earth with their feet and dig down three or more feet with their tusks. They throw sand out of the well with their trunks. When they have dug deep enough, water begins to seep into the hole. Then they take a good long drink.

*An elephant flaps its ears
in order to keep cool.*

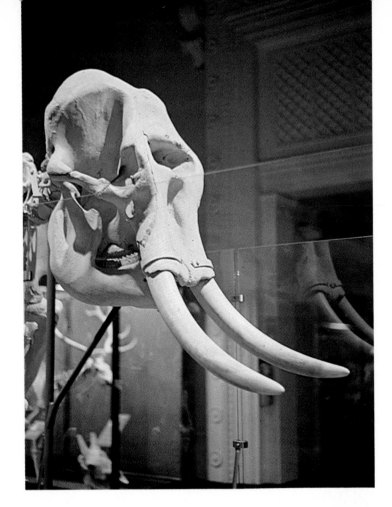

The skull of an elephant is very large but relatively light in weight.

The cheek teeth of elephants have ridged surfaces for grinding down tough plant matter.

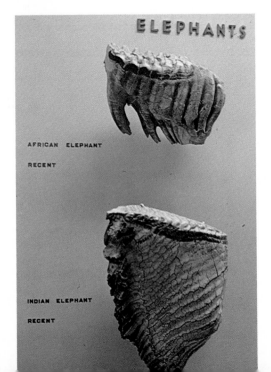

12

Tusks, Trunks, and Cheek Teeth

An elephant's head is very large, but its skull is light in weight for its size. The skull is made of spongy bone that is full of air spaces.

The long ivory tusks are special types of teeth. The tusks keep growing throughout the elephant's life. Often tusks are broken off or worn down. Elephants use their tusks for digging, protection, and play fighting. They push at the flanks of other elephants with their tusks to drive the others away. But they seldom injure each other with the tusks.

If an elephant lives long enough, its tusks can grow to be eight or ten feet long. A few tusks have measured eleven feet in length and weighed close to 150 pounds each. There is one tusk in the British Museum that weighs 226½ pounds. It is the heaviest tusk known.

Tusks are not as important to the life of an elephant as are its molars or *cheek teeth.* Elephants use the cheek teeth to grind down the tough plant food that the animal eats. The food must be ground before it can be digested.

The elephant's cheek teeth tell a unique story in the animal world. The teeth are ten to twelve inches in length and weigh eight to nine pounds. They have ridged chewing surfaces.

During a normal lifetime, an elephant grows a total of twenty-four cheek teeth. The elephant chews and grinds its food with one set of four cheek teeth, two teeth on each side of the jaw. Eventually, the teeth wear down. Then new ones grow in from the rear of the jaw. These push forward in the mouth to replace the old ones. The elephant grows six sets of cheek teeth.

The last cheek teeth grow in when the elephant is about sixty years old. Some elephants live to be seventy years old. A few live to be older. But if its last set of cheek teeth is worn down, an elephant will not be able to chew its food. It will die.

*A female elephant protects her
young by placing her trunk
and chin over its body.*

The elephant's long trunk is also very important for its survival. The trunk is part nose and part lip. It is strong and full of muscles. The elephant can turn it freely in all directions. There are more than forty thousand muscles in an elephant's trunk.

An elephant breathes through its trunk. It also tickles, scratches, rubs, pats, and smells with its trunk. When thirsty, it sucks a gallon or two of water into its trunk and squirts the water into its mouth. The elephant can push down trees, tear off bark, and lift heavy logs with its trunk. It uses the lip at the end of the trunk to grasp tiny berries, nuts, and leaves.

14

Despite its great size, an elephant has remarkable balance.

The lip at the end of an elephant's trunk is used like a finger for grasping small objects.

15

Elephants walk with an
ambling gait.

The elephant's large, soft
foot is protected by
tough toenails.

16

An elephant has large, soft feet with tough toenails. It walks on the tips of five toes. Its large feet are cushioned by great pads of tissue that help distribute the animal's great weight.

When an elephant walks, the two left legs move forward together, then the two right legs. This is called *ambling.* Giraffes, camels, and bears also amble.

In the wild, the elephant lives in warm climates. It has very little hair on its body. There is a tuft of thick hairs at the end of its tail. When its body gets too hot, the animal sweats. It might walk into a river or water hole to keep cool. It also sprays water or dust behind its ears, or flaps its ears in the air. Sometimes an elephant cools its body by throwing dust on its back. Like any mammal, an elephant will die if its body overheats too much.

When excited, angry, or threatened, an elephant might bellow, trumpet, lift its trunk, or charge. It holds out its ears as wide as it can and waves its trunk back and forth. Several elephants might move together to form a great wall.

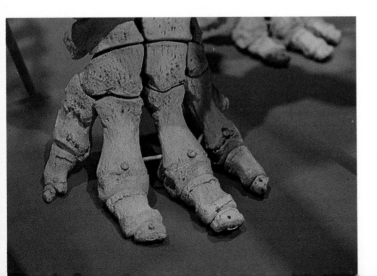

These foot bones show how an elephant walks on the tips of its toes.

17

Friendly elephants greet each other by wrapping trunks together.

Female elephants have the longest pregnancies of any mammal. *Gestation*—the period of time the mother carries her baby in her uterus —is twenty-one months. The newborn calf weighs about two hundred pounds and stands three feet tall. Like all mammals, it nurses on its mother's milk until it is old enough to eat solid food.

Young elephants do a lot of playing while they are growing up. They run around and chase one another. They fight and push at each other with trunks, heads, and tusks. Smaller elephants usually give way to larger, older ones. Serious fighting rarely takes place.

When the young bulls are eleven to thirteen years old, the female leaders drive them out of the herd. From that time on, the young bulls follow the herd with the older bulls. They return to the herd only during mating periods.

Elephants in the same herd have strong bonds of affection. They greet each other by wrapping trunks together. Sometimes one puts the end of its trunk into another's mouth. They protect and try to help injured members of the herd. When an elephant dies, others might stand around its body for days, making sad, moaning sounds.

An elephant drinks through its mouth, not through its trunk.

There is a popular myth that elephants go to a common graveyard to die. This is not true. Elephants die from accidents, injuries, diseases, starvation, or whenever they are killed by human hunters. These things could happen anywhere. Some African elephants remove the tusks and bones of dead elephants and place them in piles elsewhere. Some elephants cover the bodies of dead elephants with branches and leaves.

19

The cheek teeth of the ancient mastodon rose from the jawbone like the cheek teeth of modern elephants.

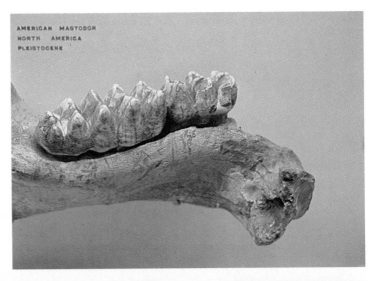

The skeleton of a modern elephant consists of skull, neck bones, large rib cage, and long leg bones. Its ancient relatives were often larger animals.

The skull and tusks of a North American mastodon. Some tusks were sixteen feet long.

Ancient Relatives

Mammoths and *mastodons* were ancient relatives of modern elephants. They roamed northern Europe and North America more than a million years ago. Their teeth, tusks, and fossil bones have been dug out of gravel pits and bogs. Some of these animals stood fourteen feet tall at the shoulders and had tusks sixteen feet long.

Many mammoths and mastodons lived in cold, arctic climates as recently as ten thousand years ago. Some preserved bodies have been found in frozen bogs in Siberia and Alaska. Food was still in their mouths. Yellowish-brown woolly fur covered their bodies. Patches of long, thick, black hair hung from their cheeks and their sides. Their ears were smaller than the modern elephant's and were covered with fur. Primitive people used spears and bows and arrows to hunt these animals.

Mastodon tusks, bones, and teeth have been found in gravel pits and bogs near Chicago.

Mammoth skeletons also have been
found in the Chicago area and
in other parts of the world.

*The white or square-lipped
rhino has a wide, square lip.*

Rhinoceroses—Horns on the Nose

The rhinoceros is another large mammal with thick skin and very little hair. Like the elephant, it is a *herbivore,* or plant eater.

There are several species of rhinoceroses. Some live in the forests and on the savannas in Africa. Others live on the grasslands, on the bamboo hillsides, or in the tropical forests of Asia.

Black rhinos and *white rhinos* are native to Africa. Both species are really slate gray in color. The name "white rhino" probably comes from the Afrikaans word *wyd,* which means "wide." The white rhino has a wide, square lip. It is also called the *square-lipped rhino.* Its mouth is suited for feeding on grasses. White rhinos roam the plains of Africa, grazing entirely on grasses.

The black rhino has a hooked lip and is also called the *hooked-lip rhino.* It lives near rivers and large lakes. It often browses at night. It uses its hooked lip like a finger to pull shoots, leaves, and twigs from bushes. It usually eats thorny and woody plant food.

The black rhino is usually seen alone or with one or two other rhinos. Its senses of hearing and smell are very keen. While walking, it often turns its nose into the wind. It can be easily provoked by a strange smell. The animal is known for its unpredictable actions.

Sometimes the smell of another animal seems to anger the black rhino. Then it attacks. It lowers its head, stamps its feet, charges, and strikes with its horns. Sometimes it strikes its victim several times.

*Can you recognize a rhinoceros
by its large eye and thick skin?*

The white or square-lipped rhino is less aggressive than the black rhino. It does not like to fight as much. When a white rhino is alarmed, it simply curls its tail over its rump and trots away.

Rhinos must eat a great deal of tough plant food. Vegetable matter is more difficult to digest than meat and requires much more chewing. Rhinos grind down grass, leaves, and woody plants with their cheek teeth.

A rhino's horns grow on its nose. Most African rhinos have two horns. Asian rhinos have one or two horns. A few rare rhinos have three horns.

The rhino's horns are not true horns. They do not rise from bone as do horns of a goat or an antelope. The rhino's horns are formed by hard hairlike or hooflike material matted thickly together. If a horn is torn off, a new one begins to grow. In zoos, the horns are often worn down and polished. The animals keep rubbing them against walls, fences, or rubbing posts.

Rhino horns form from hard hairlike or hooflike material.

Most rhinos are grazing animals.

A rhino uses its lip
to take food.

A baby rhino displays
early horn growth.

The feet of a rhino are thick and sturdy. They support a body weight of about two tons. Each foot has three toes. The rhino walks on the tips of its toes. For short distances, it can run at speeds of twenty to thirty miles per hour.

Large, thick-skinned animals are often pestered by insect bites and parasites. A rhino's hide is bitten by many flies, ticks, and other insects. While rhinos wallow in water holes, turtles bite out and eat ticks from the skin of the big animals.

When courting, the male rhino walks near the female with short, careful steps. He swings his head from side to side. The female might snort and charge at him with her horns. So he gallops away. But he always circles back to come near her again. A long period of butting and playful fighting might occur before the animals mate.

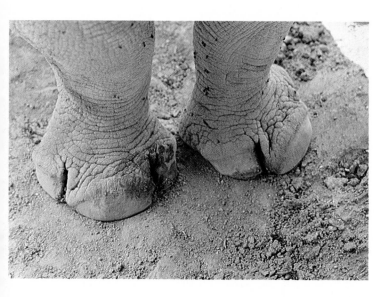

A rhino has three toes on each foot.

Rhinos in zoos live comfortable lives. Their plant-food diets are carefully regulated.

Most large mammals have very long pregnancies. They usually give birth to only one baby at a time. Small mammals, such as mice and hamsters, have short pregnancies and many babies in each litter. The female rhino is pregnant for about eighteen months. The young calf suckles on its mother's *udder* or mammary glands until it can eat solid food.

In the wild, rhinos make common dung heaps. When a rhino takes its daily walk to the water hole, it usually passes a dung heap. It sniffs at the heap, jabs at it with its horns, and then deposits its own dung on the pile. Some rhino dung heaps are more than four feet high and twenty feet across.

Rhinos live for thirty to forty years. In zoos, some of them live longer. A rhino generally lives a peaceful life. But when startled, threatened, or provoked, it can cause quite a battle. Perhaps this is why a group of rhinos is called a *clash*.

A rhino skull with front ridge plate, large nasal bone, and large cheek teeth.

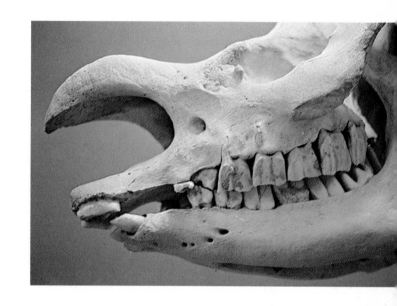

The baby rhino follows its mother wherever she goes.

*Female hippos are very
protective of their young.*

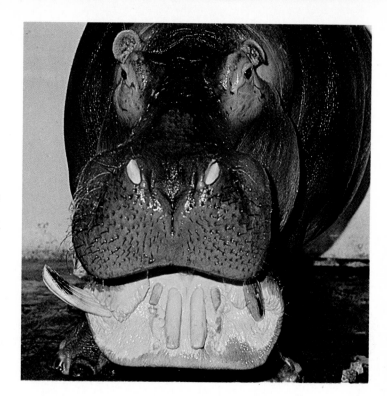

A hippo's tusks sometimes grow at odd angles.

Hippopotamuses—Overgrown Pigs

The word *hippopotamus* means "river horse." But hippos are more closely related to pigs. They are plump, round animals with short legs and webbed toes. Many adult hippos weigh up to three or four tons. They can live to be forty years old in the wild. Some live longer in zoos.

Hippos live in the rivers of Africa. During the hot days, they spend most of their time sunning on sandbanks or resting in the water. Hippos swim and dive well. They have large lungs. An adult hippo usually stays underwater without breathing for two to six minutes. If it wants to, it can stay under longer. It might even take a long walk along the bottom of the river.

At night, hippos leave the river and walk many miles along *hippo roads.* Generations of hippos have followed the same paths to feeding grounds for hundreds of years. These paths have become deep, sunken roads.

33

A baby hippo hides under its mother. A newborn hippo weighs about sixty pounds.

Hippos feed mainly on marsh grass that is high in protein. They also eat shrubs, leaves, and fallen fruit. A single hippo can eat as much as 130 pounds of plant matter during one night's feeding. It might not return to the water until shortly before dawn.

Females are leaders of the *schools,* as groups of hippos are called. They are very protective of their young. Adult males live outside the main school of females and young. If a female wants to visit a male or graze alone, another female will take care of her calf until she comes back.

After a pregnancy of eight or nine months, a female gives birth to one calf. The baby hippo is born in the water. It must swim to the surface to fill its lungs with air for the first time. The baby also nurses in the water, but can stay underwater for only twenty to thirty seconds. Then it must come up for air again.

34

Sometimes the calf will stand on its mother's back as she floats in the water. A calf stays close to its mother for several years, until it is large enough and old enough to be on its own. If the young calf strays from its mother while grazing on land, it could be killed by a lion or a leopard that is hiding in the grass.

If a mother sees that her baby is threatened by a crocodile in the river, she will attack. She will crush the crocodile with her strong jaws and teeth and drag it under the water until it drowns.

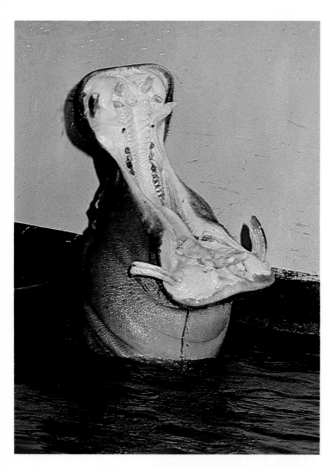

Hippos yawn a great deal. Often, the hippo yawn is an act of aggression.

*A healthy pygmy hippo
has a glossy skin.*

*The foot of a hippo
has four toes. The
animal walks on the
tips of its toes.*

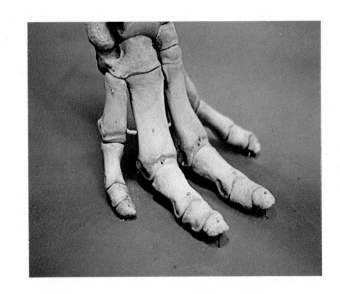

A hippo skull with tusks, jaws, cheek teeth, and eye sockets.

Hippos have thirty-eight to forty-two teeth. Their sharp cutting teeth and their wide cheek teeth are used for biting off, chewing, and grinding down tough marsh grass and other water plants. The large ivory tusks are used in slashing and fighting. The tusks continue to grow throughout the life of the hippo. The tusks must wear down against each other or break off before they grow too large for the hippo's mouth. Sometimes the tusks grow at odd angles. Then it is hard for the hippo to chew.

Adult male hippos often fight fiercely over who will live in a certain part of the river. Roaring and splashing, two males might rear up out of the water and attack each other with mouths wide open. They slash at each other with their tusks. The fight might last for hours. Finally, one hippo retreats. Both animals are usually injured by the slashing tusks.

The pygmy hippopotamus is the only other species of hippopotamus. It is found only in Liberia, Sierra Leone, and the Ivory Coast. These countries are in West Africa.

The pygmy hippo is a much smaller animal. It weighs about six hundred pounds as an adult. Pygmy hippos do not live in groups. They usually live alone or in pairs. Pygmy hippos spend most of their lives on land, in dense, swampy forests. They spend much less time in the rivers than do the large river hippos. The female pygmy hippo has a pregnancy of about seven months.

Hippos have an unusual habit of sweeping and scattering their dung with their tails. This is seen often at zoos and in the wild. This African folk story tells why Kiboko sweeps dung with his tail. *Kiboko* is the Swahili word for "hippo."

God created Kiboko and ordered him to cut grass for the other animals. When Kiboko arrived in Africa and found out how hot it was, he asked God's permission to stay in the water during the day and to cut grass only at night. God was not eager to say yes. He was afraid Kiboko would spend all his time eating fish. So Kiboko spreads out his dung with his tail each day to show God that there are no fish bones in it.

*A pygmy hippo enjoys taking
a mud bath.*

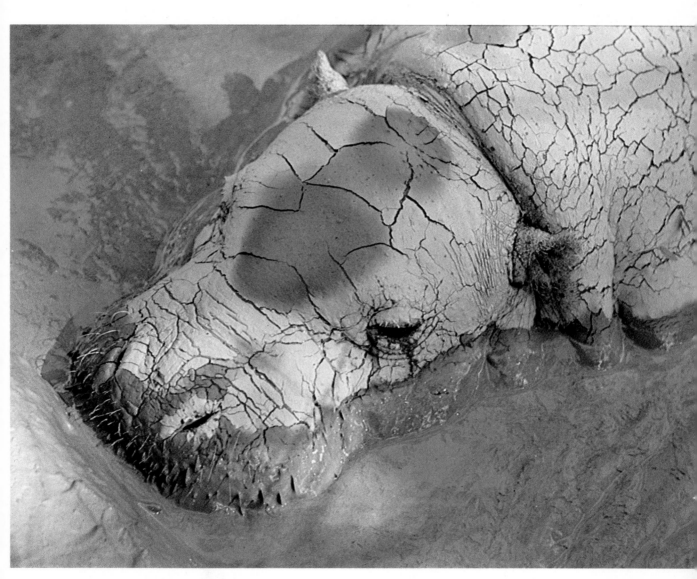

*Mud helps keep a thick-skinned
animal cool and protects
its skin from insect bites.*

An American tapir skeleton
with skull, neck bones,
rib cage, leg and foot bones.

A Malayan tapir's markings
help conceal the animal
while it rests in the
shadows.

*The tapir's flexible trunk,
like the elephant's,
is part nose and part lip.*

Tapirs—More Long Noses

Tapirs existed fifty to sixty million years ago. One million years ago, tapirs lived in most parts of the world. But today, tapirs are found only in the thick jungles of Central and South America, Thailand, Sumatra, and Malaysia.

Tapirs do not live in groups or herds. They tend to live alone except when mating or when a female is raising a single young. Tapirs are shy, quiet animals. They are not aggressive and are not known to attack other animals.

During the day, tapirs rest in dense jungle thickets. At night, they swim and dive in rivers. They feed on grass, leaves, swamp plants, and fallen fruit. They do not eat meat.

The largest species, the Malayan tapir, has an average length of eight feet and a weight of six hundred to seven hundred pounds. Its short hair is black and white. Its colors and markings help to hide the tapir in jungle shadows from tigers on the hunt.

The American tapir is a smaller animal. Its hair is dark brown or reddish in color. It is sometimes preyed on by jaguars.

Gestation is twelve to thirteen months. Malayan and American tapirs have similar colors and markings when born. Their coats are dark, and marked with yellow and white stripes and spots. The pattern begins to change in each species when the young are six months old.

Both Malayan and American tapirs have four toes on their front feet but only three toes on their hind feet. The neck skin at the shoulders is almost one inch thick. The nose and upper lip form a short, flexible trunk. The tapir uses its trunk to pluck leaves and branches from shrubs. Tapirs have forty-two to forty-four teeth.

Hunting Big Game

Primitive people hunted large, wild animals for food and for other things they needed to survive. They used the skins for clothing and shelter. They used the bones as tools.

Modern big-game hunters kill large animals for sport and to collect trophies. Some hunters shoot elephants for their tusks. Others kill tigers for their coats. Many hunt rhinos for their horns.

On hunting safaris in Africa, men and women shoot at big game with high-powered rifles from fifty to one hundred yards away. A professional game hunter stands alongside with even bigger guns to back them up.

Many hunters like to tell stories about the so-called "dangerous" animals they faced. But most wild animals are not dangerous unless injured, threatened, or provoked. They usually try to run away from human beings.

Once, a hunter in Zaire shot a large bull elephant in the head. The bullet did not kill the elephant. He ran off, wounded. Many days later, the bull saw a tourist who was trying to take pictures of him. The bull charged and slapped the tourist down with one blow of his trunk. The bull kneeled on the tourist's body and gored it with a tusk. Then, strangely, the bull covered the tourist's body with branches and leaves.

Game wardens tracked down the bull and killed it. They found that the bull's head was full of infection and pus. This had caused the animal great pain. If the elephant had not been wounded, he probably never would have attacked a human being.

In Africa, Masai and Boran teenage boys used to hunt elephants, rhinos, and lions with spears to prove their manhood. A group of boys, nearly naked and each armed with two spears, tracked lions with mongrel dogs.

When a lion was spotted, the boys approached cautiously and threw their spears. The first boy to draw blood was called the bravest. He was awarded the lion if it was killed. Often, one of the boys was killed or seriously injured by the wounded lion.

Who is braver—the African boy with a spear or the big-game hunter blasting away with a gun?

In most nations, hunting big game is now illegal. Many animals are endangered species, and their numbers are dwindling. Governments protect these animals to help ensure their survival.

At times, when some animal populations grow too large, hunting is permitted to regulate the populations. Only a limited number of animals is killed.

Most safaris are now conducted for the purpose of photographing animals, not for killing them.

Glossary (as the author used the words)

aggression   readiness to fight or attack

amble   type of walk where the two left legs move forward together, then the two right legs

ancestors   animal species of the past from which modern animals descended

browsers   animals such as elephants that eat the leaves and branches of trees

digestion   ability of an animal to dissolve and break down food that nourishes it

domesticated   tame animals that live with people and are useful to them

gestation   pregnancy; period of time a mammal grows in its mother's uterus or womb before birth

grazers   animals such as hippos that feed on grass and other plants close to the ground

herbivore   plant-eating animal

mammal   animal that nurses its young with milk

mammary glands   female mammal's organs that produce milk for its young

naturalist   student of animals, their behavior, and where they live

nurse   suckle and feed on milk from the mother's mammary glands

pachyderms   thick-skinned mammals such as elephants, hippos, rhinos, tapirs, and pigs

parasites   ticks, lice, mites, and other tiny insects that live on or dig into the skin of large mammals

predator   animal that hunts, kills, and eats other animals to survive

44

*Does a giraffe wonder why
an elephant is so short?*

pregnancy	gestation; period of time a mammal grows in its mother's uterus or womb before birth
prey	animals hunted, killed, and eaten by predators
savanna	large, dry grassland plains in Africa with scattered shrubs, bushes, and trees
species	group of animals with common characteristics
survival	ability of animals to stay alive
territory	area where an animal feeds, breeds, raises its young, and defends its own kind
uterus	womb or organ of a female mammal in which a young animal develops and is nourished before birth

45

INDEX

About the Author

Don Arthur Torgersen is an author, poet, editor, and producer. He was born in Chicago, attended Chicago public schools, and received his higher education at the University of Illinois, University of Hawaii, and University of Chicago. During the Korean War, he enlisted in the U.S. Navy and was engaged in naval communications and electronics. Mr. Torgersen has written and produced documentaries, educational filmstrips, anthologies, textbooks, children's stories, wildlife and animal behavior stories, and audiovisual programs for government and industry. He lives in a Chicago suburb with his wife, Kathleen, and three young sluggers named Scott, Dana, and Guy. His other activities include giving lectures and poetry readings, piano playing, enjoying opera and classical music, traveling, photography, mountain climbing, skiing, sailing, and managing a boys' baseball team. Mr. Torgersen has developed the Animal Safari Nature Library to introduce animal lovers and young naturalists to the wonderful animal kingdom, the basic terms and classifications in zoology, and the fascinating aspects of animal behavior.

About the Photographer

Lee Trail is a professional photographer and photo-journalist who lives in Champaign, Illinois. She was born in Chicago, attended the University of Chicago Lab School, and received her higher education at the University of Illinois. Widely traveled, Ms. Trail has done documentaries and educational photography in the United States, Canada, Europe, Africa, Central and South America, and the West Indies. She has also done commercial photography for advertising and industry. Her interest in animal photography began on fieldwork studies for the University of Illinois Natural History Survey. When not on assignment, Ms. Trail is active in equestrian jumping competition, gourmet cooking, scuba diving, flying, and falconry.